Relax and Unwind
An Adult Coloring Book

M. MacDowell

Copyright © 2017 by M. MacDowell
All rights reserved. No part of this publication may be reproduced, distributed, or transmitted in any form or by any means without the prior written permission of the publisher, except in the case of brief quotations embodied in critical reviews and certain other noncommercial uses permitted by copyright law.

Printed in the United States of America

I would like to dedicate this book to my mom who always believes in me even when I am not very believable. I don't say it enough but I hope you know I love you very much.

Coloring has been proven to reduce stress and relieve symptoms of anxiety. There is no correct way to color – everyone should find their inner artist and create their own masterpiece.

Each image was printed on one side only to avoid bleed through onto the next picture. I suggest using a piece of paper or thin cardboard in between pages for the best results.

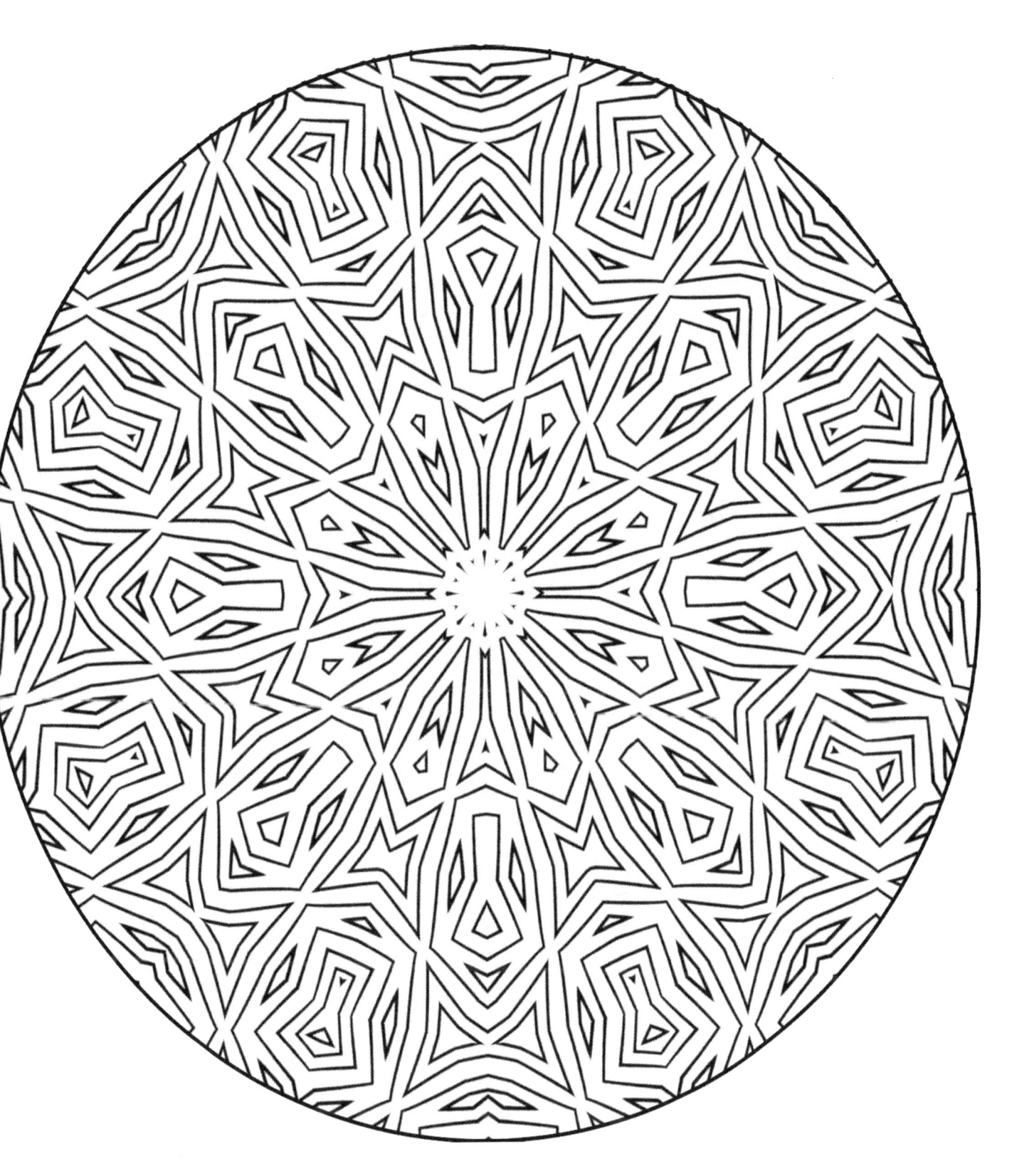

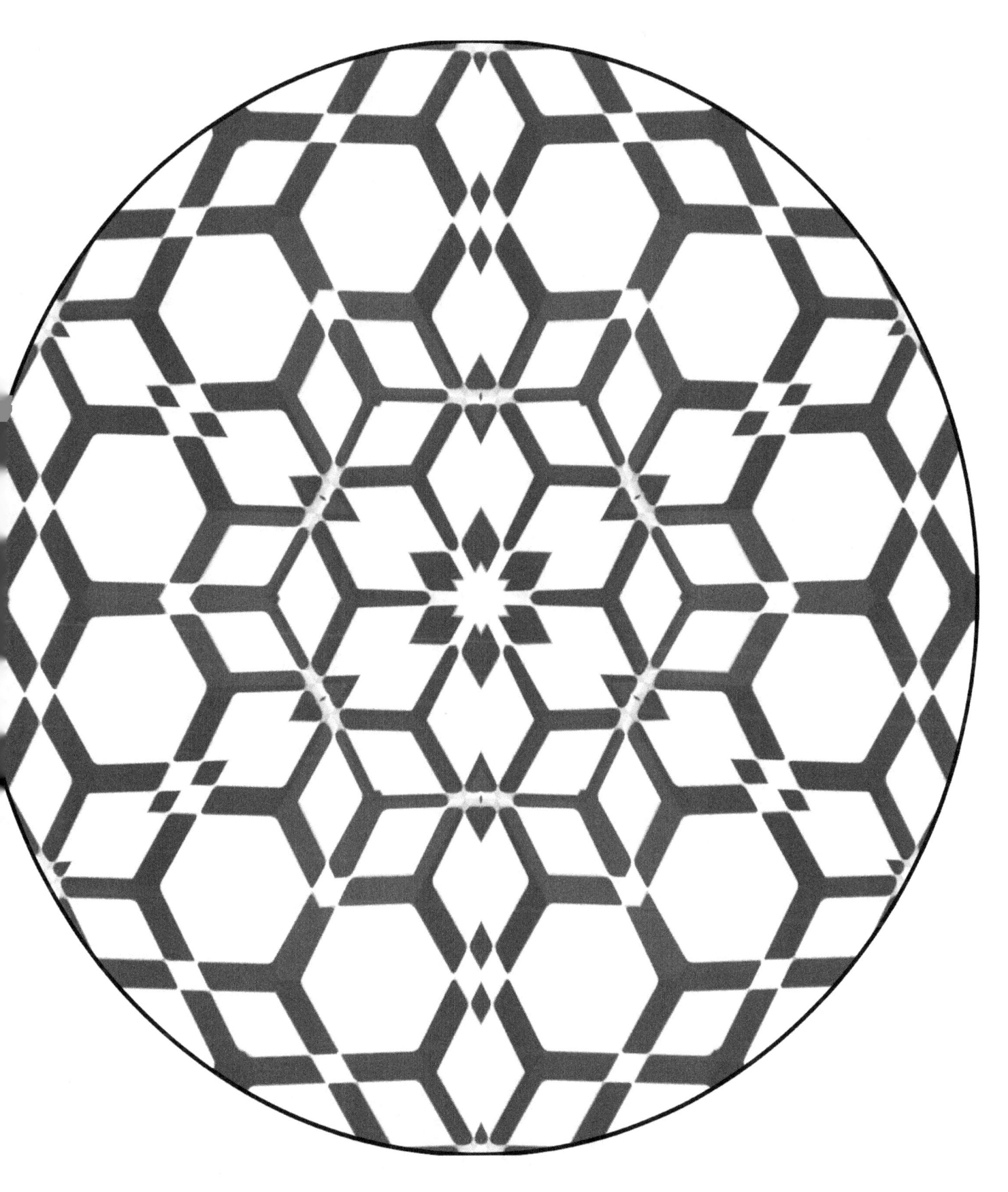

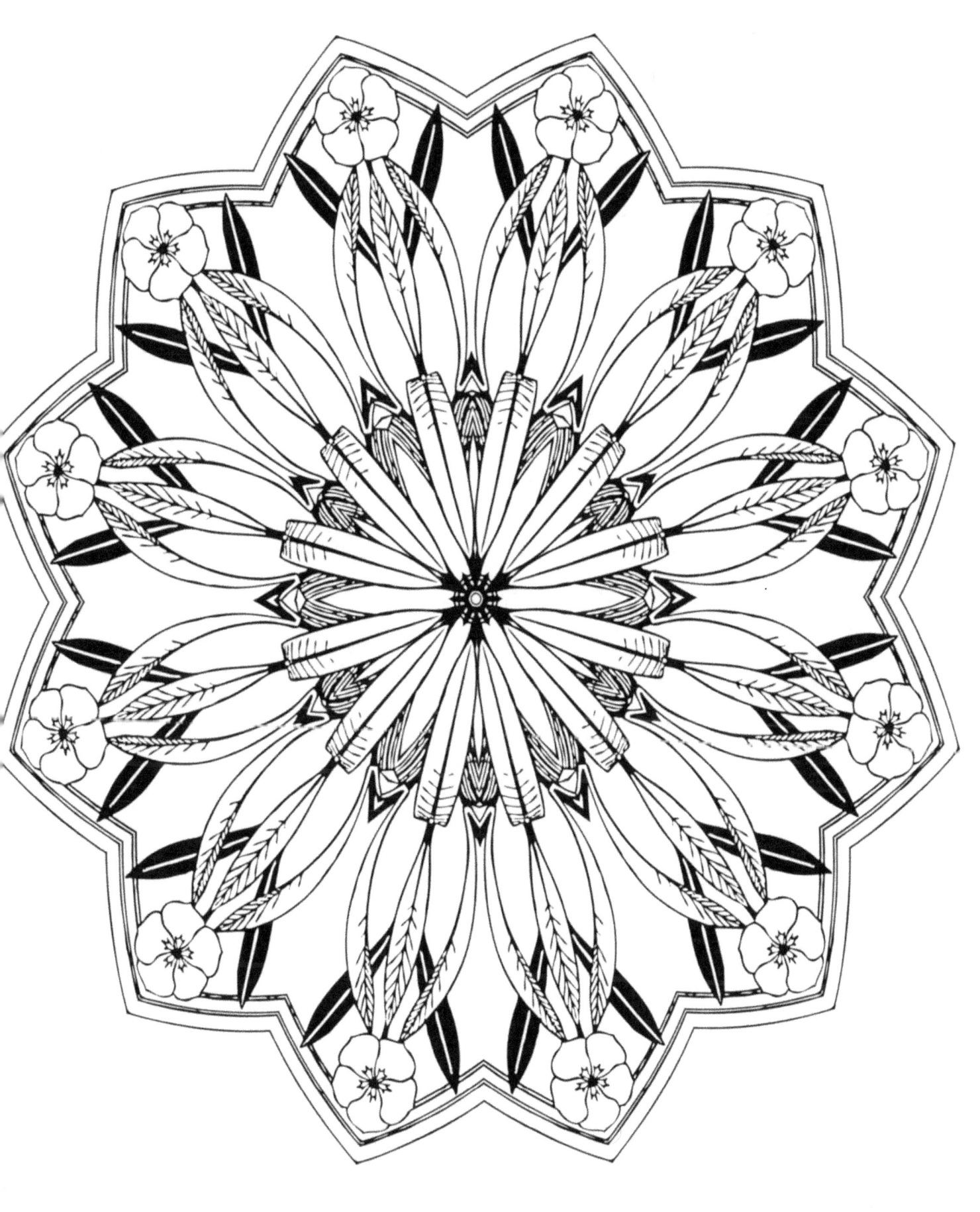

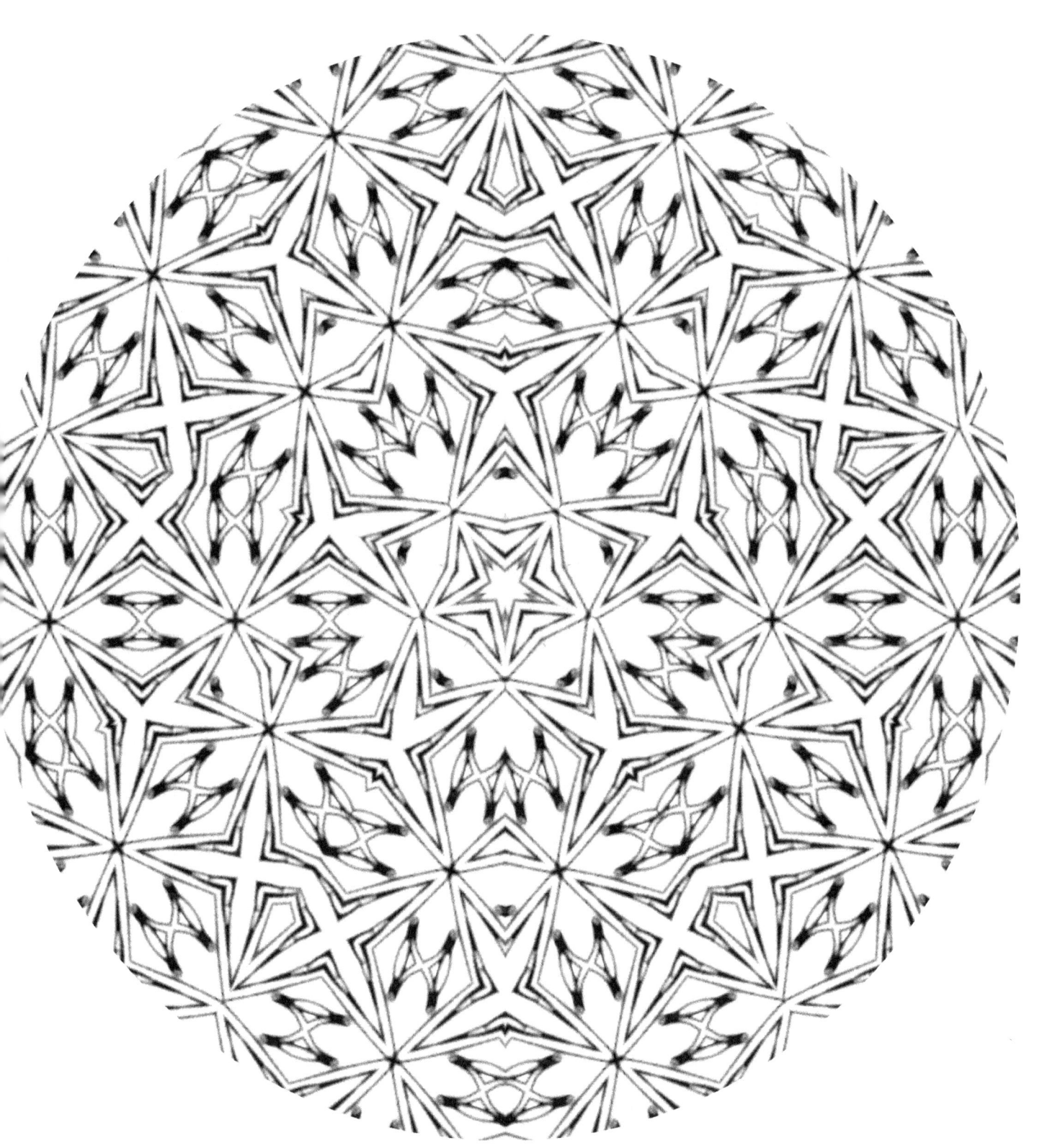

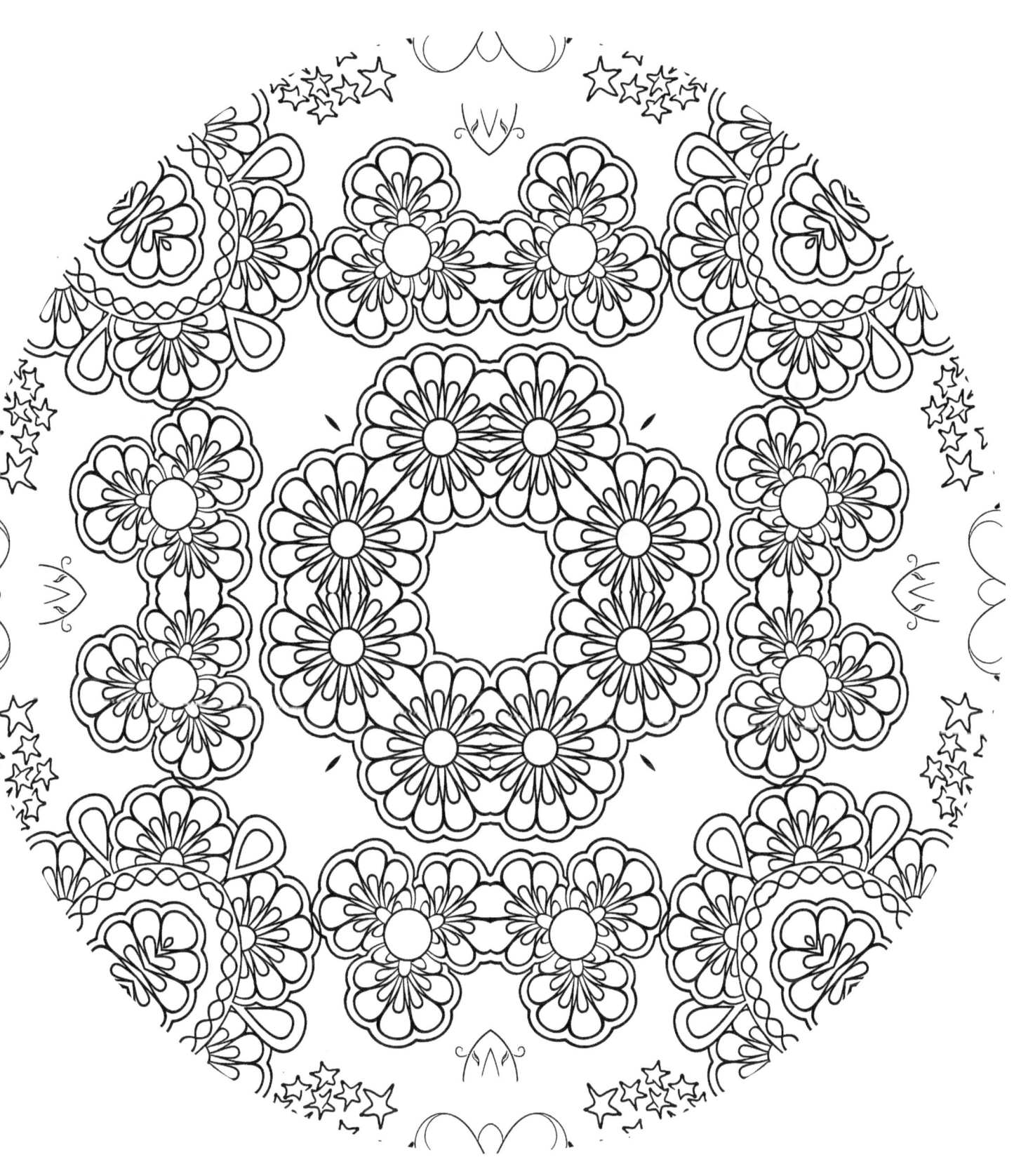

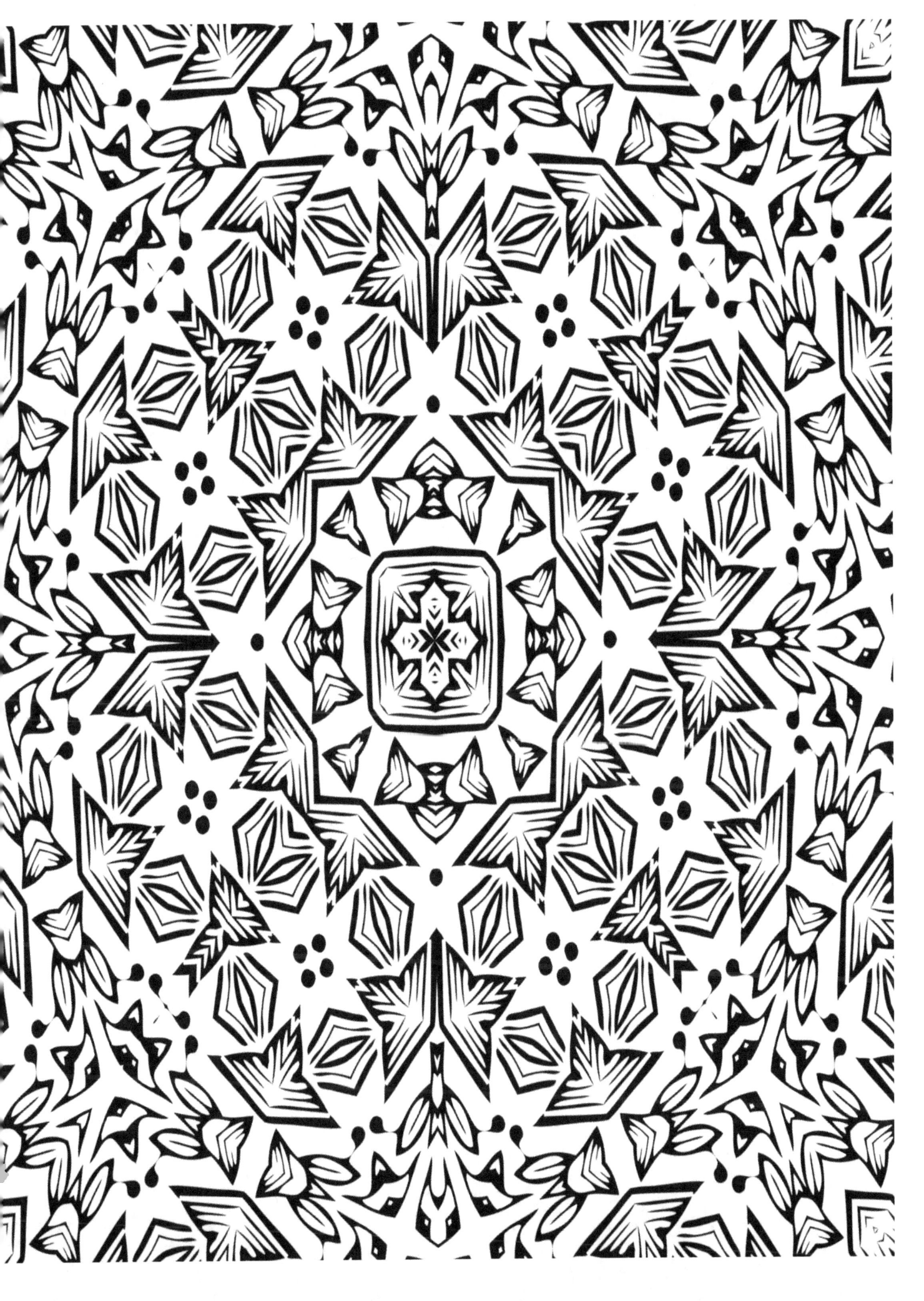

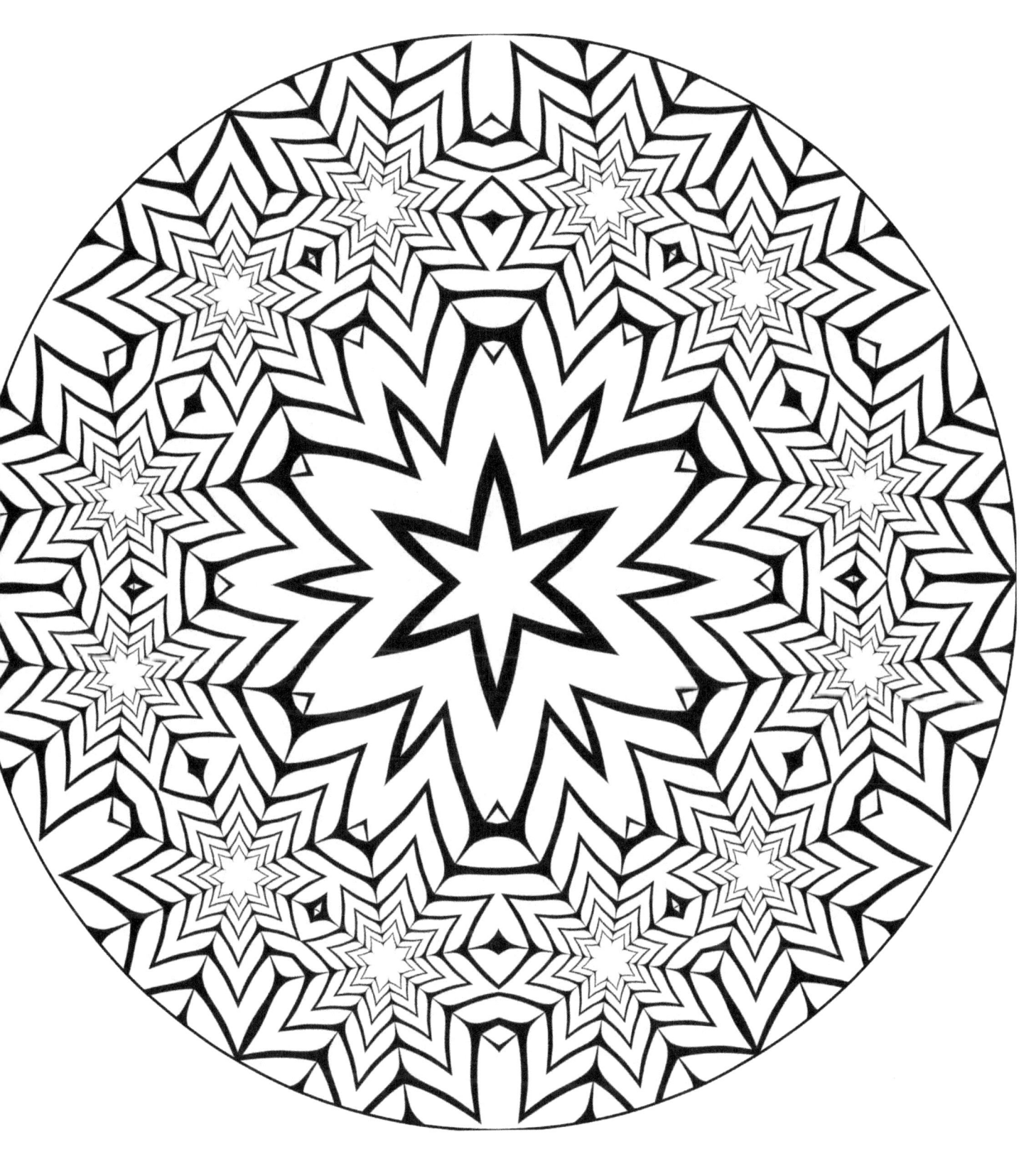

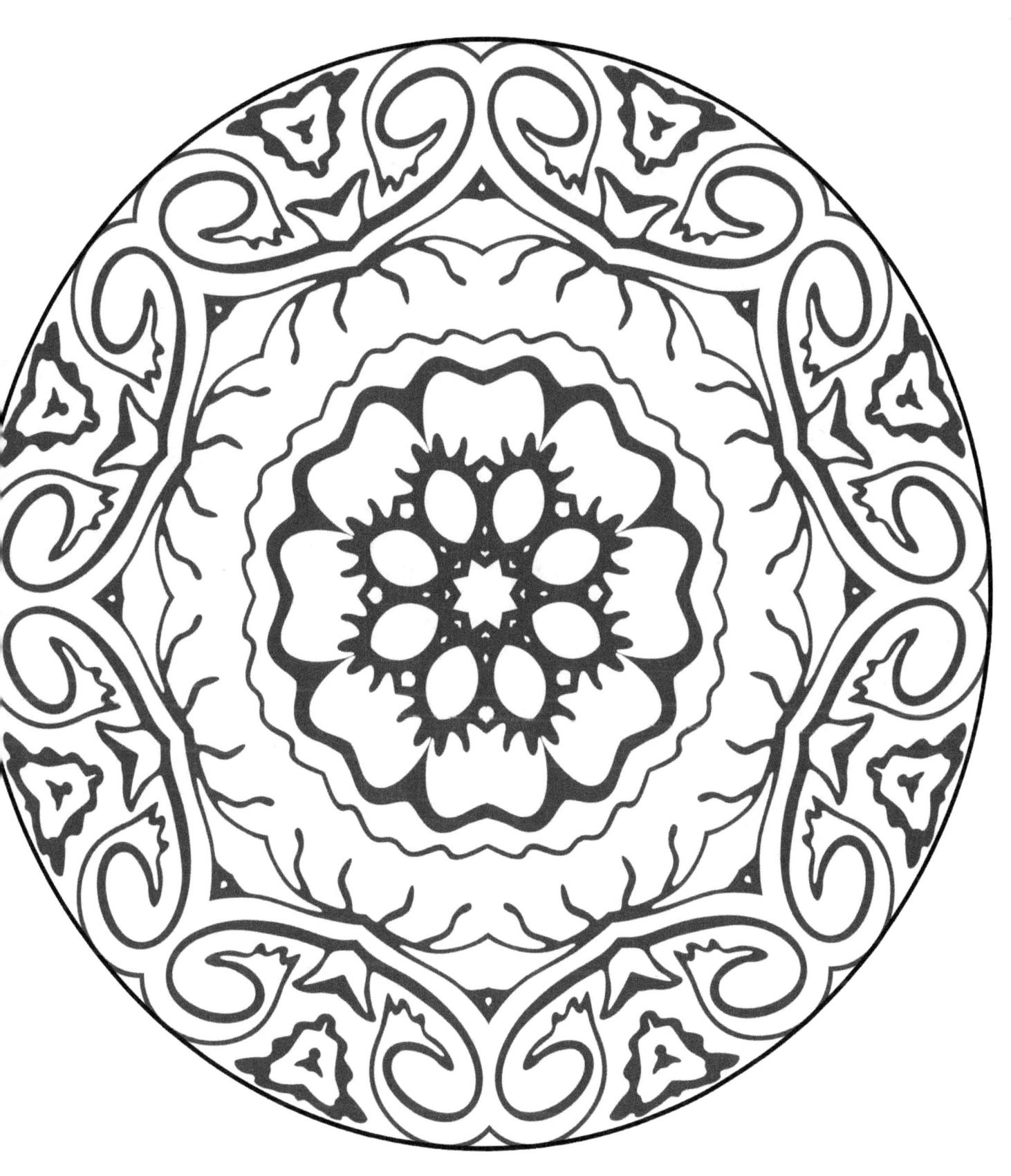

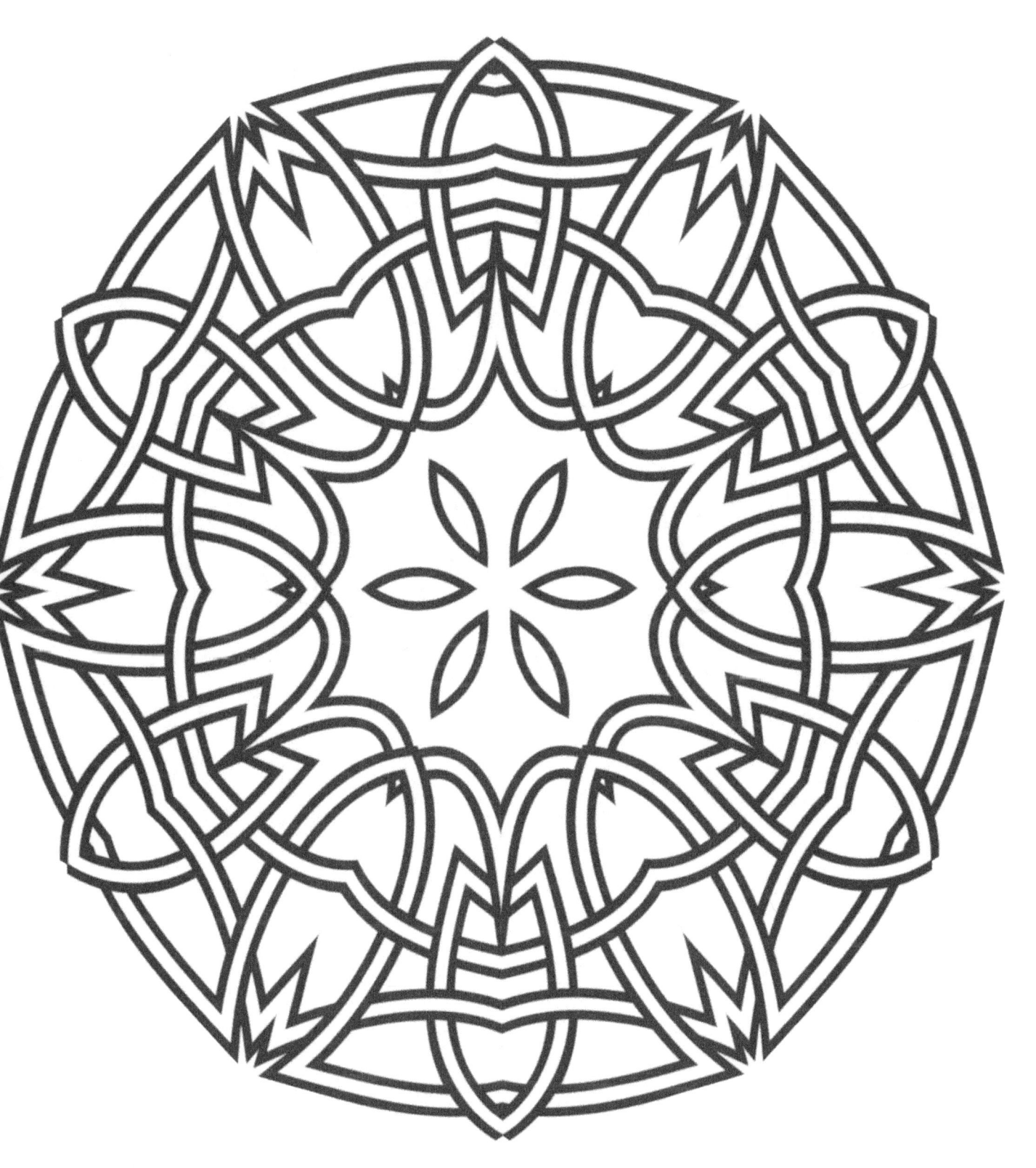

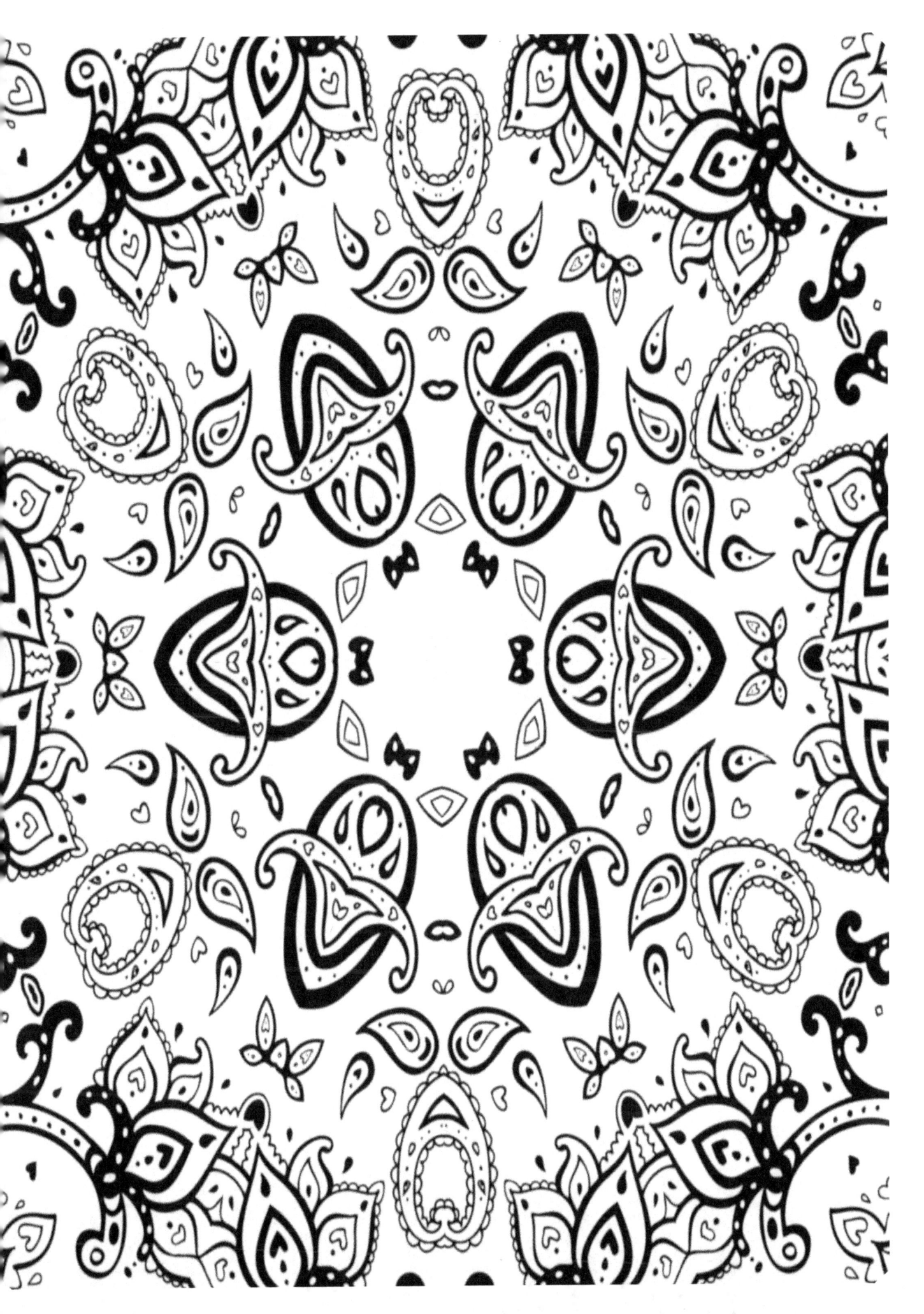

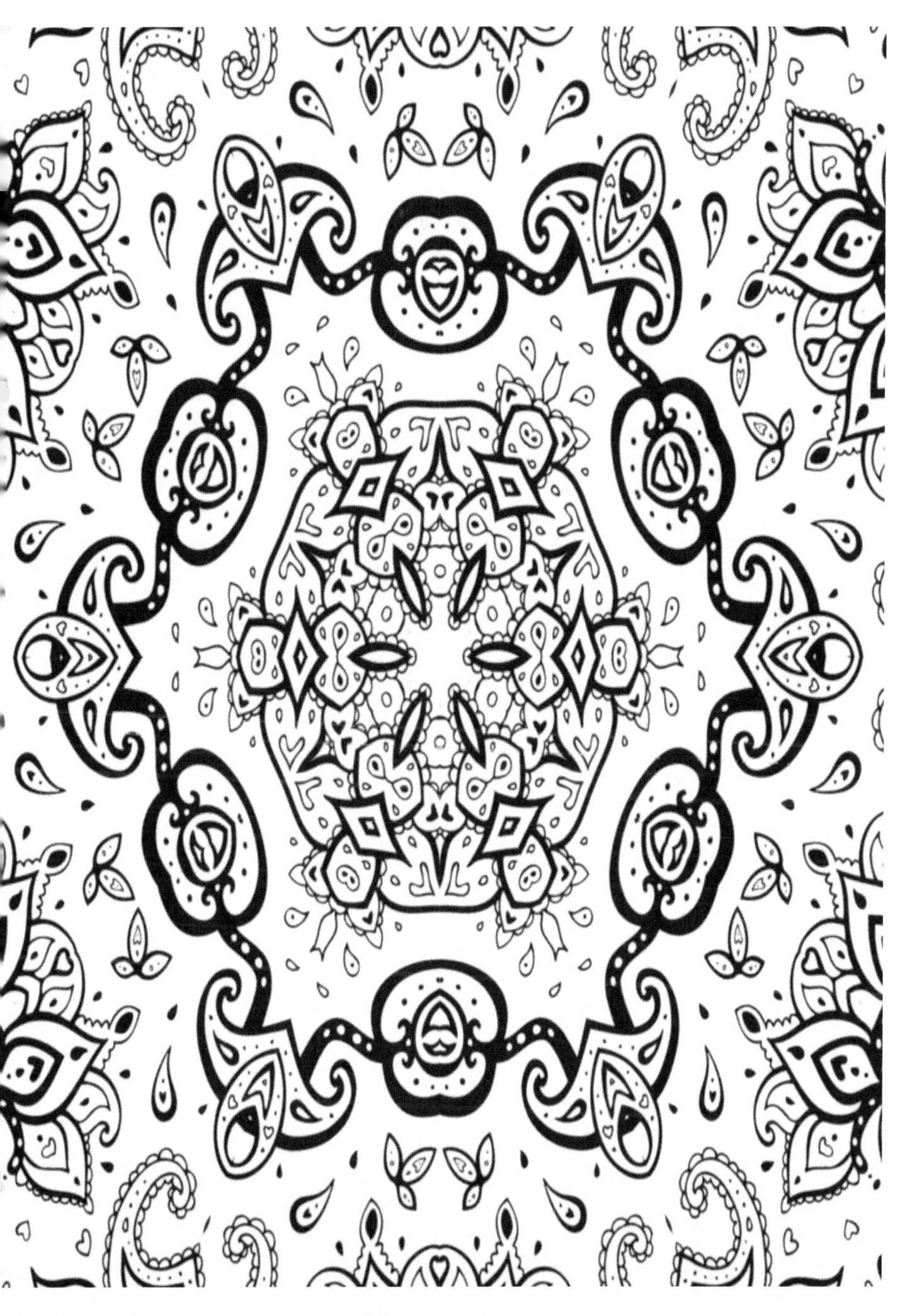

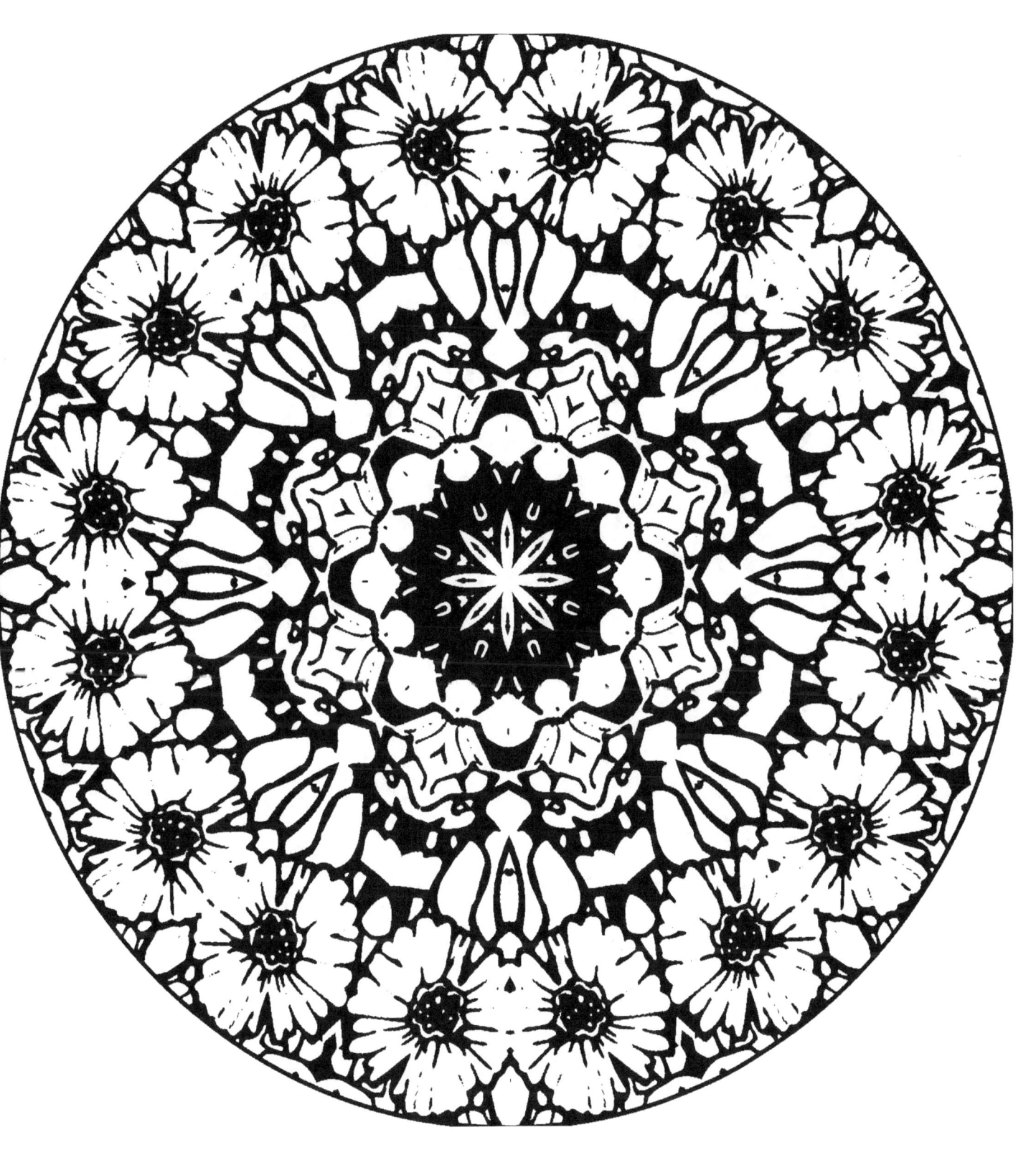

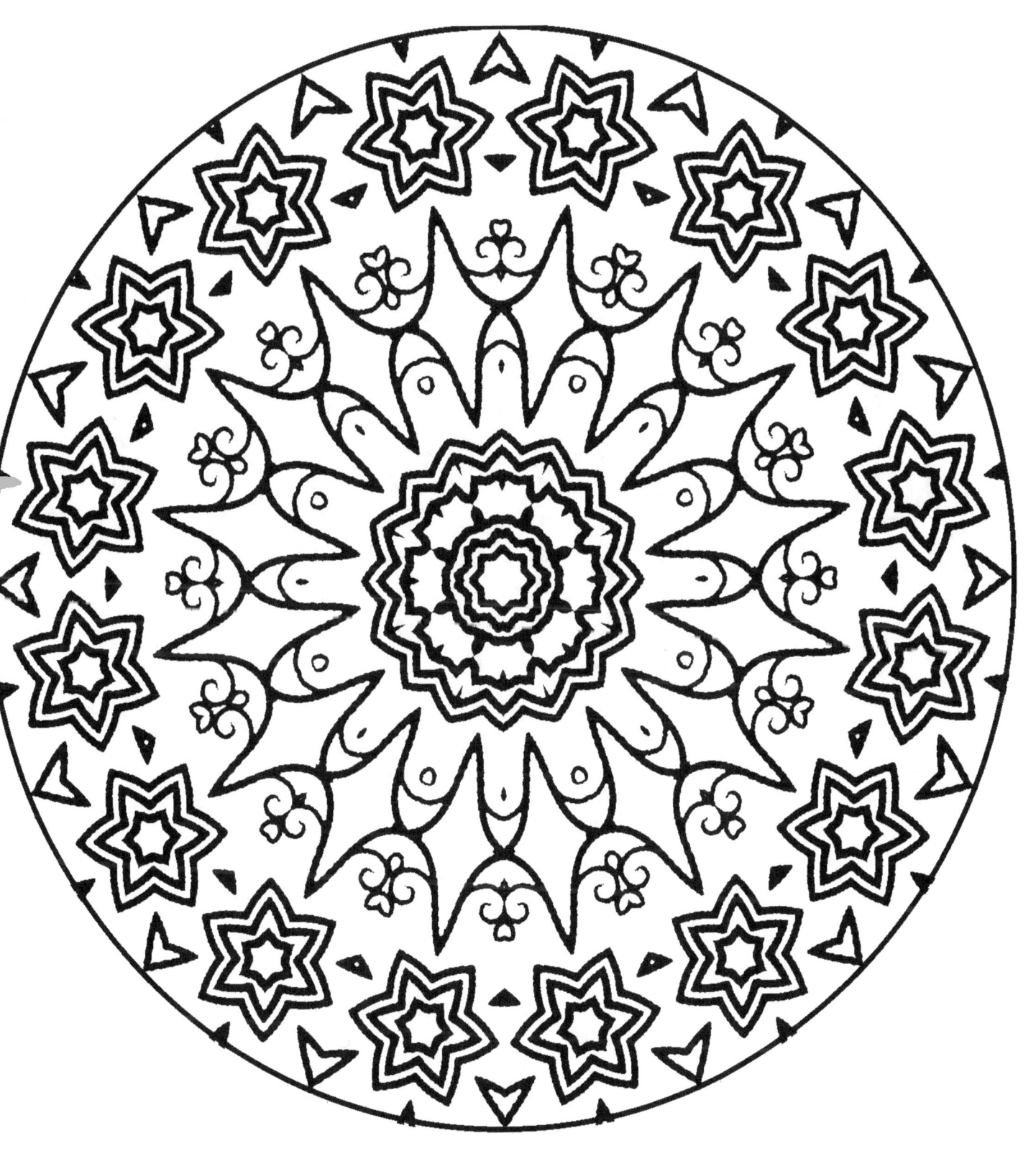

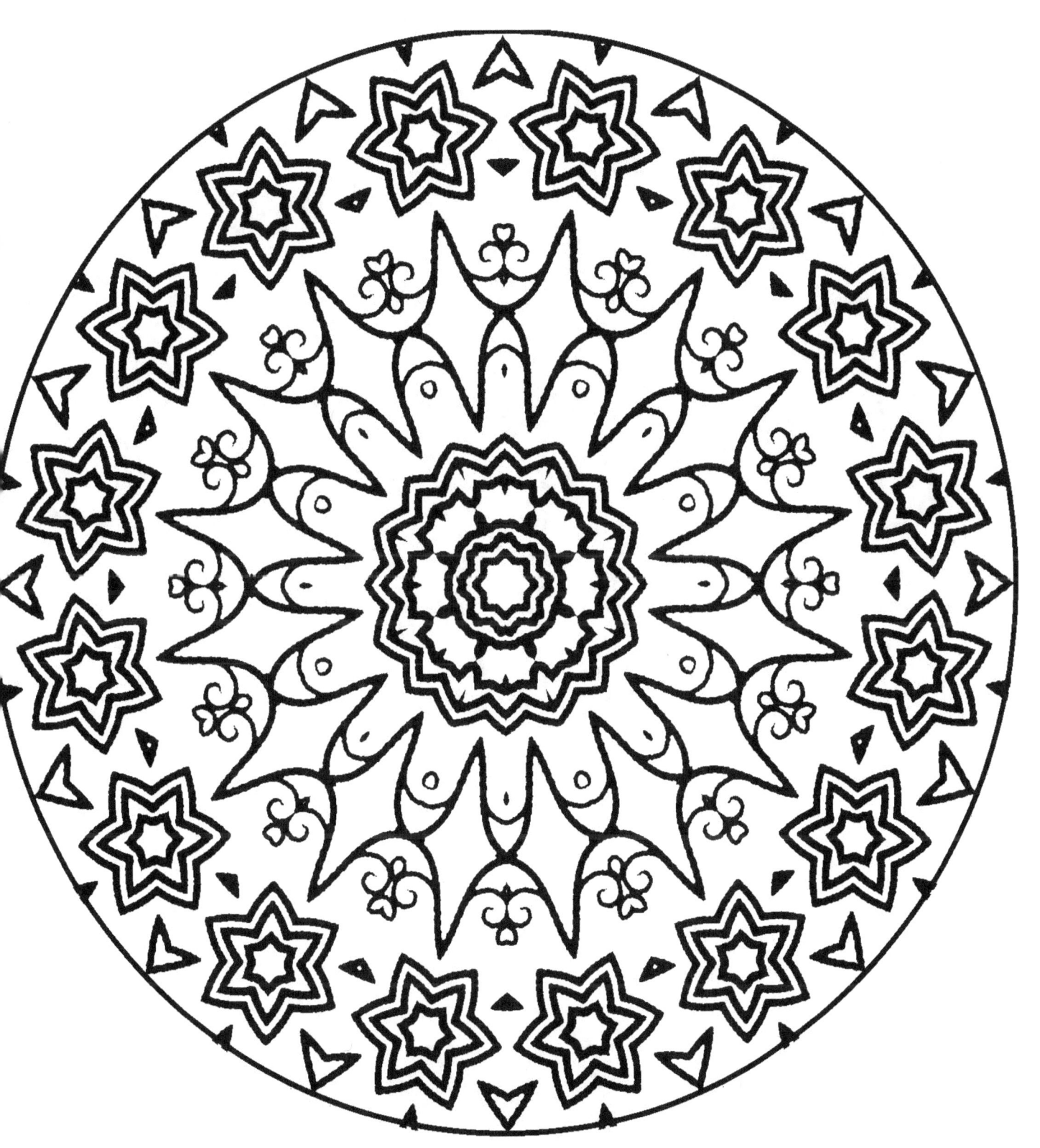

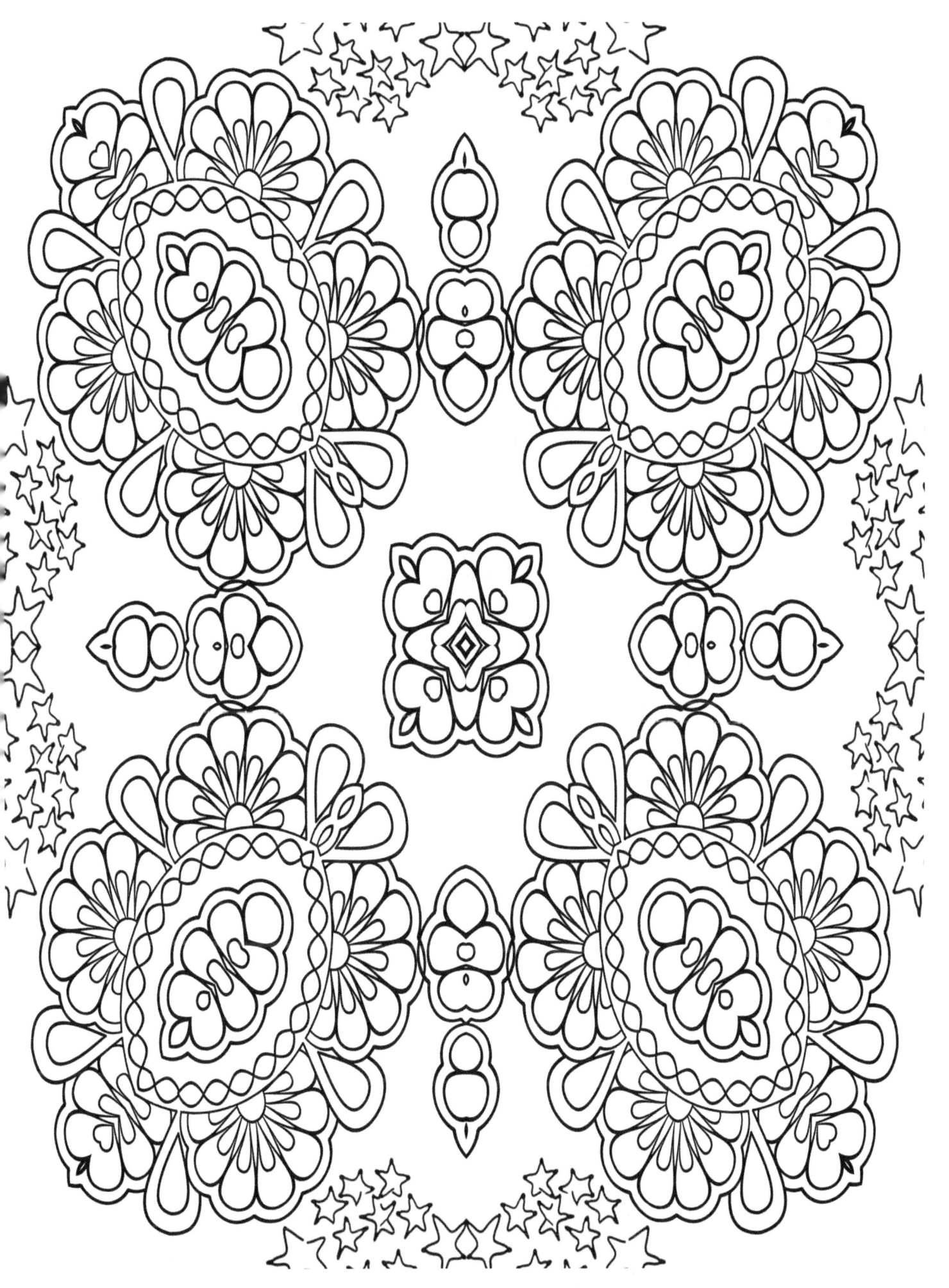

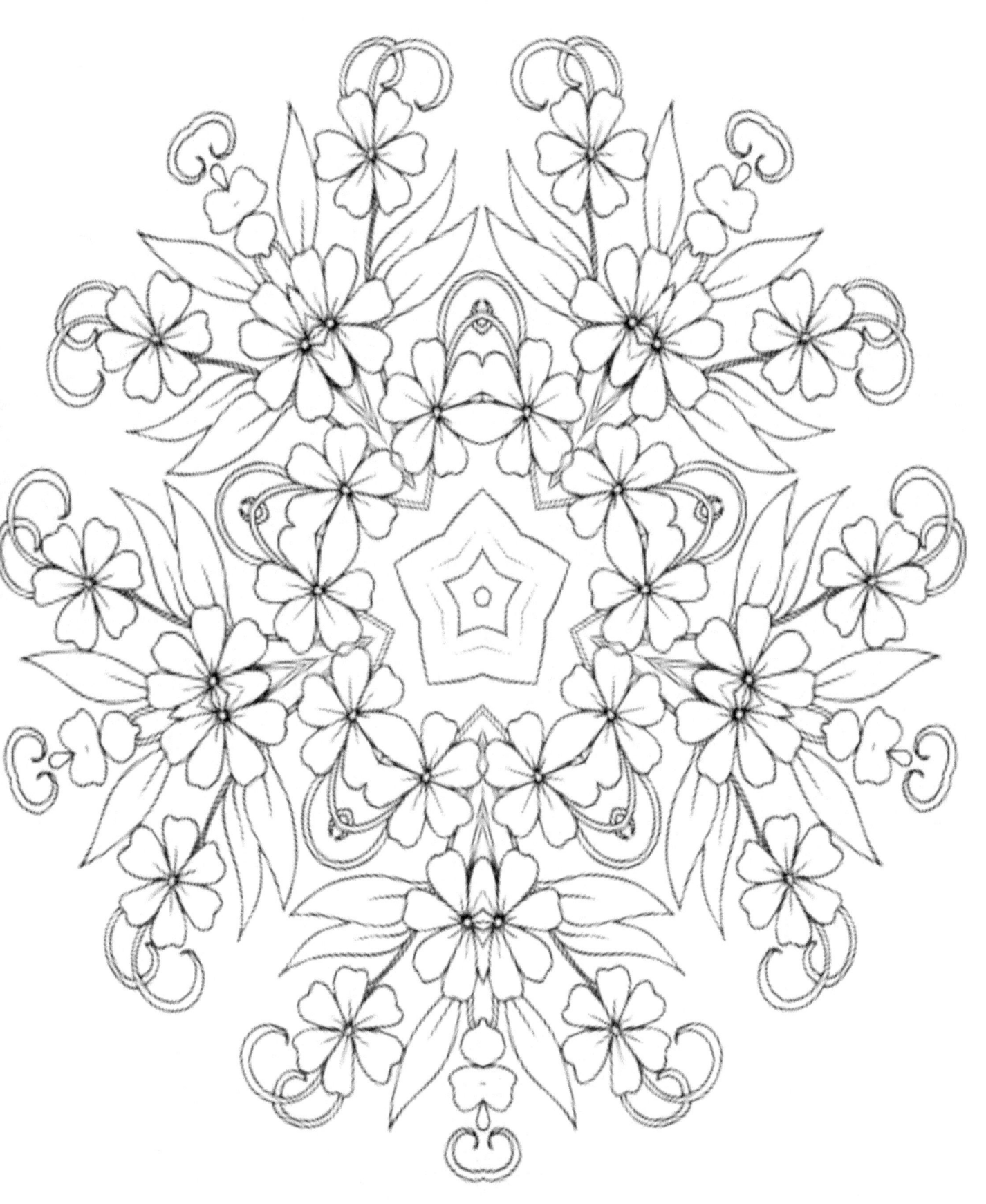

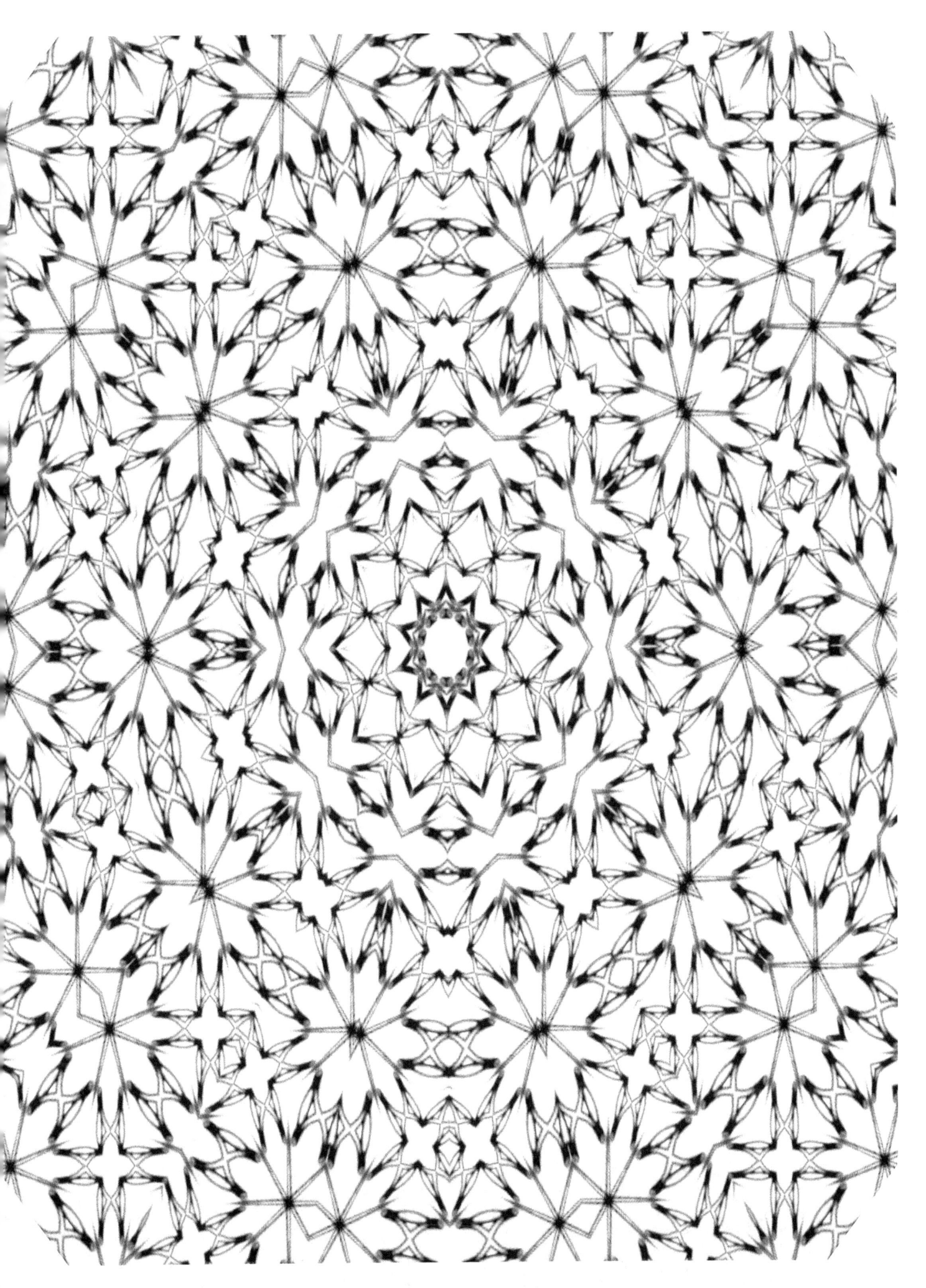

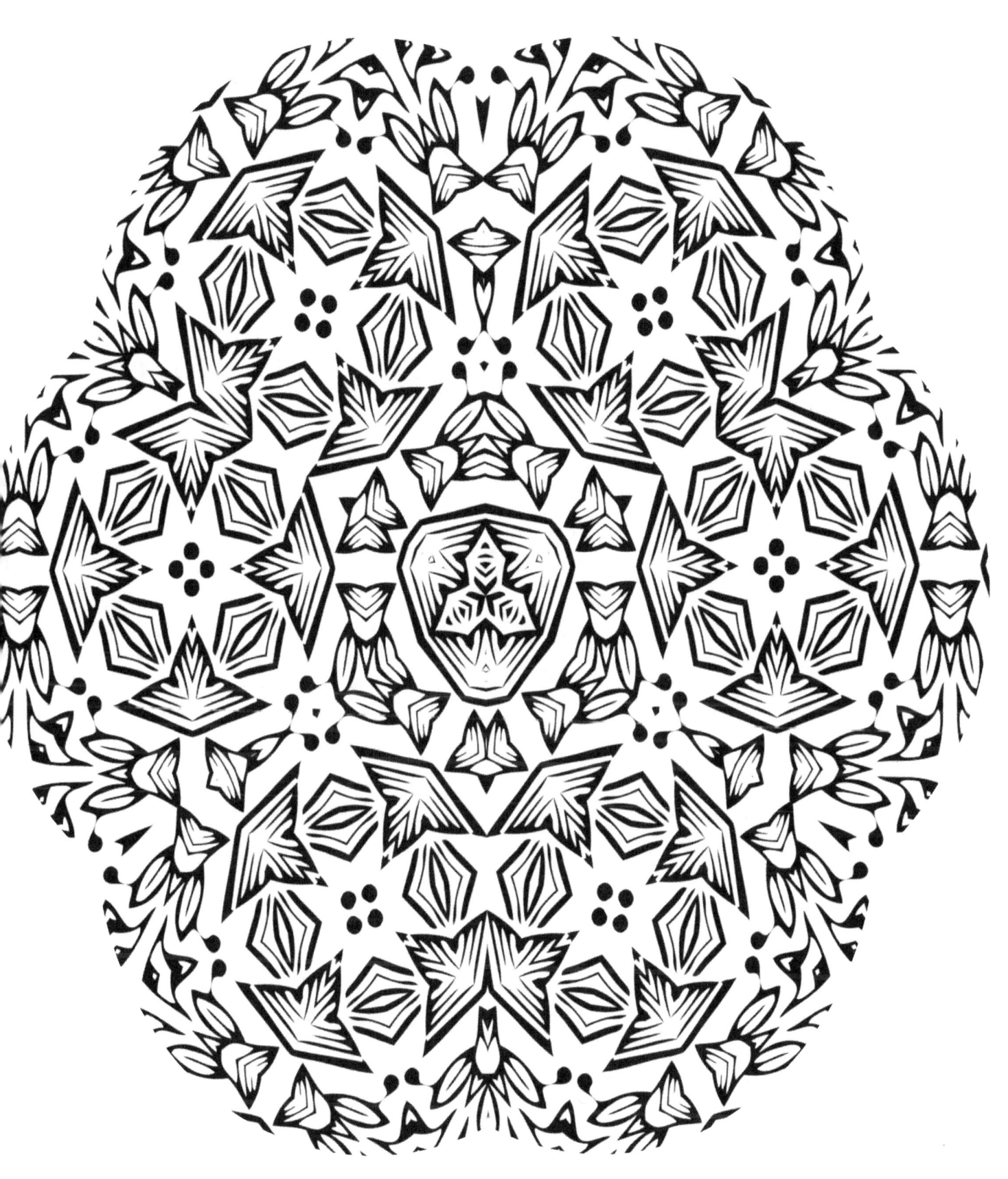

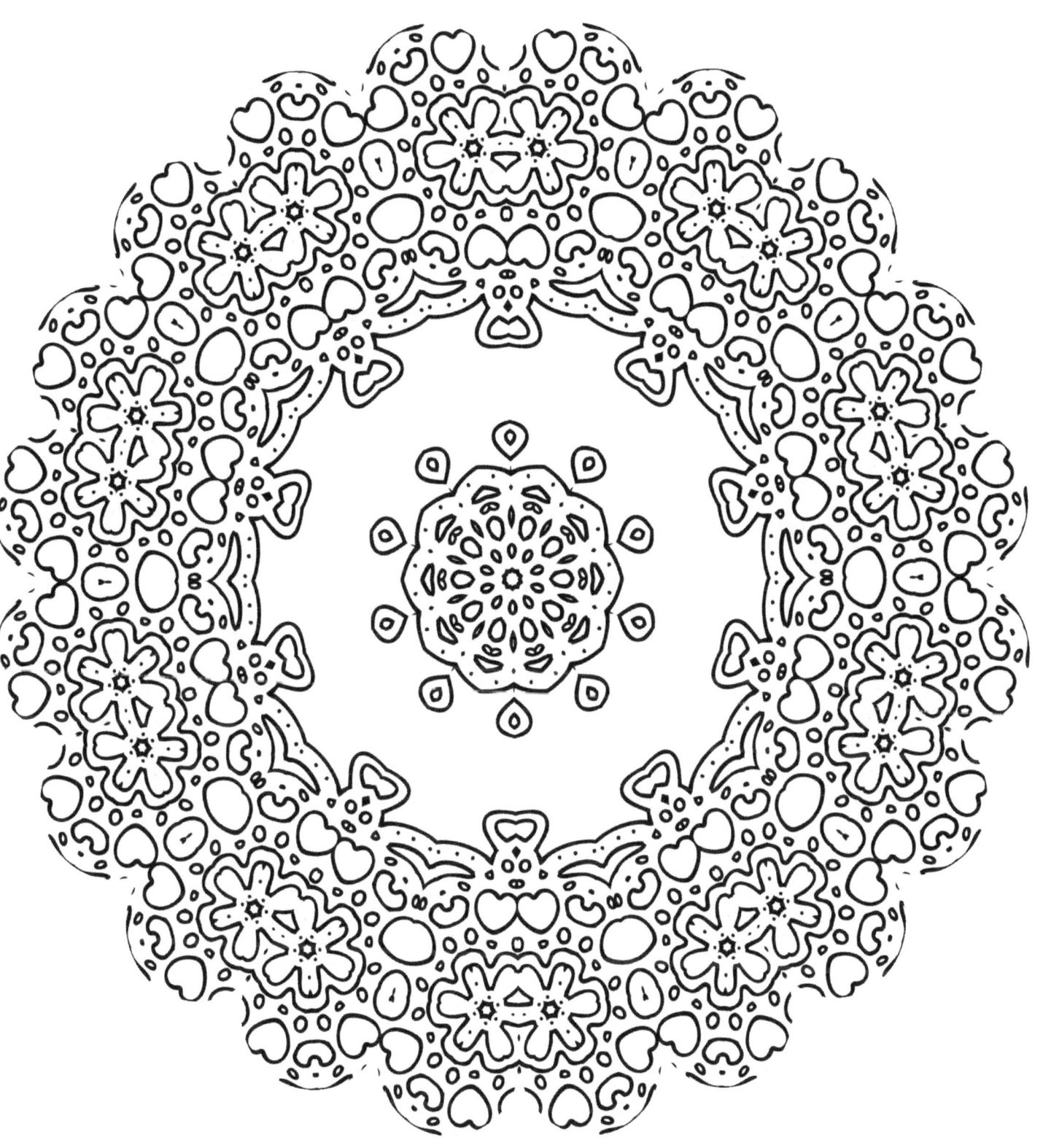

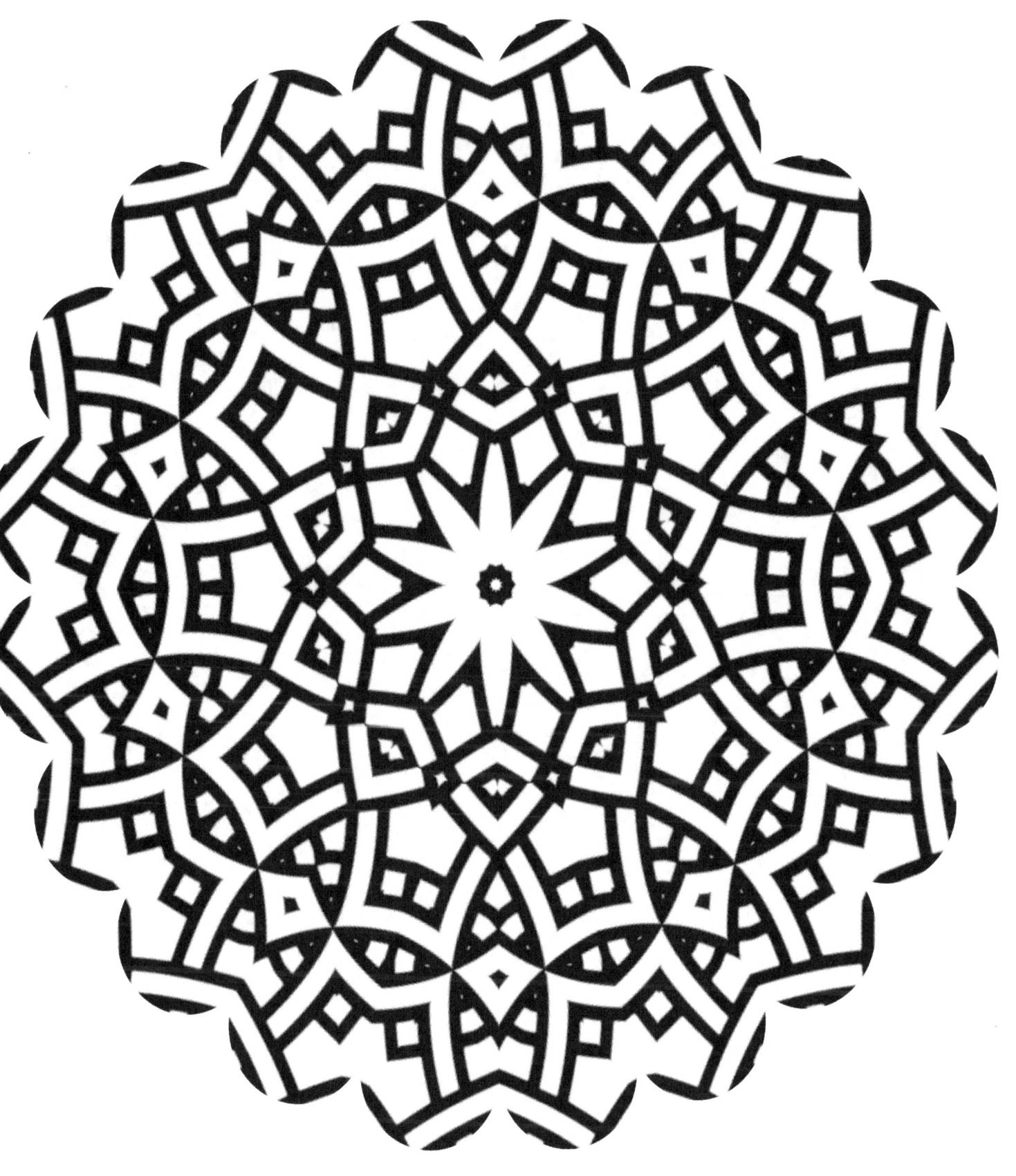

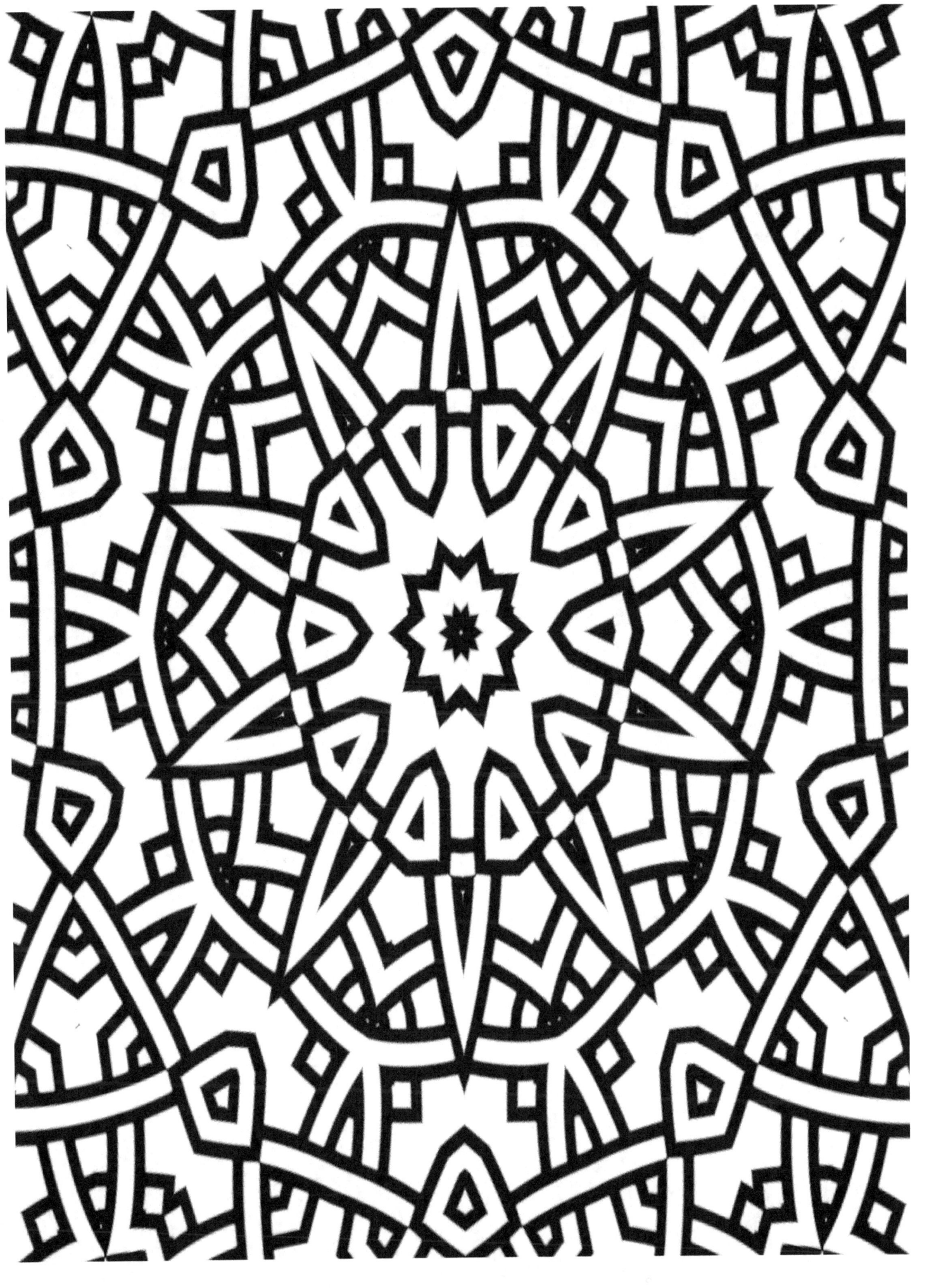

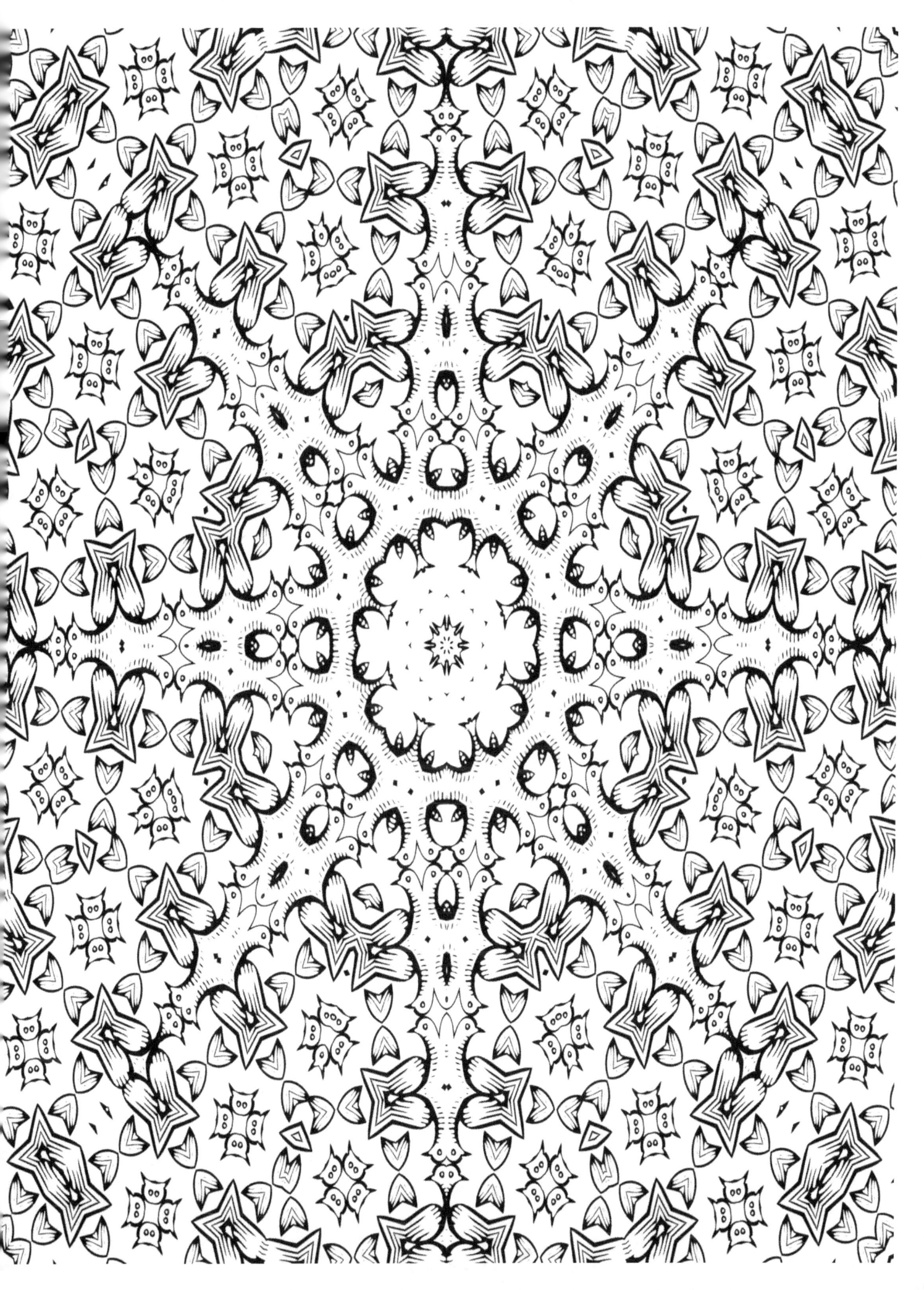

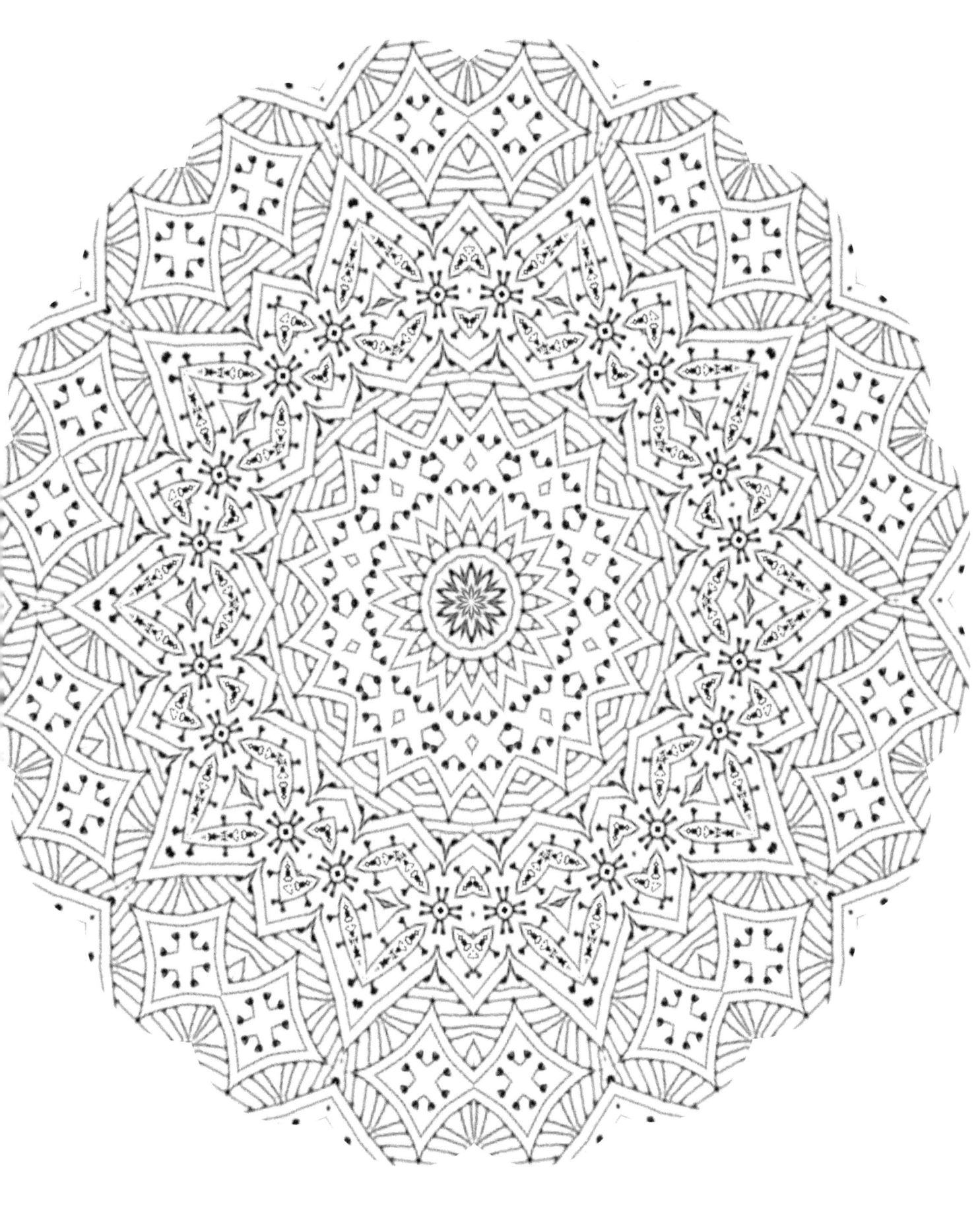

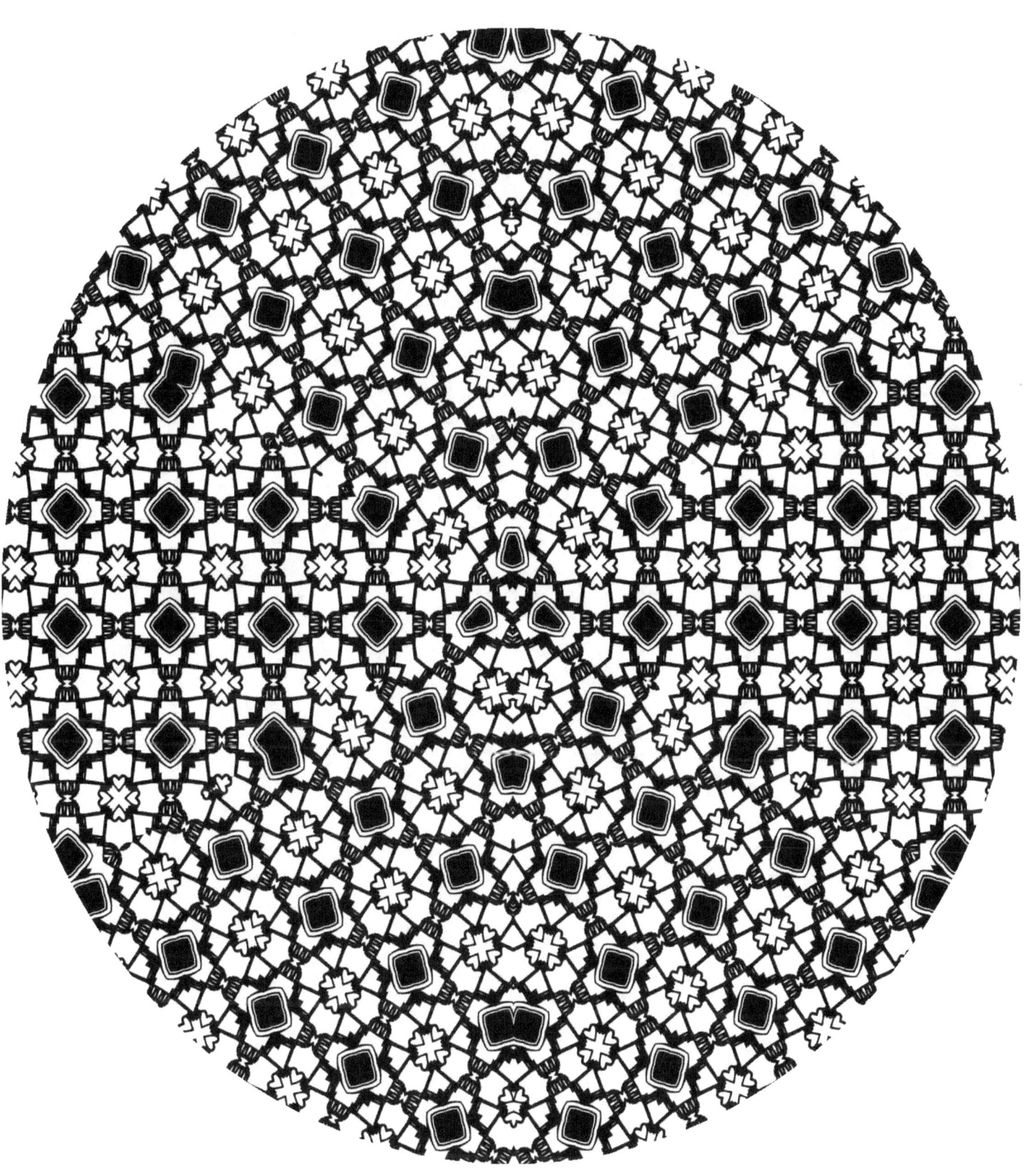

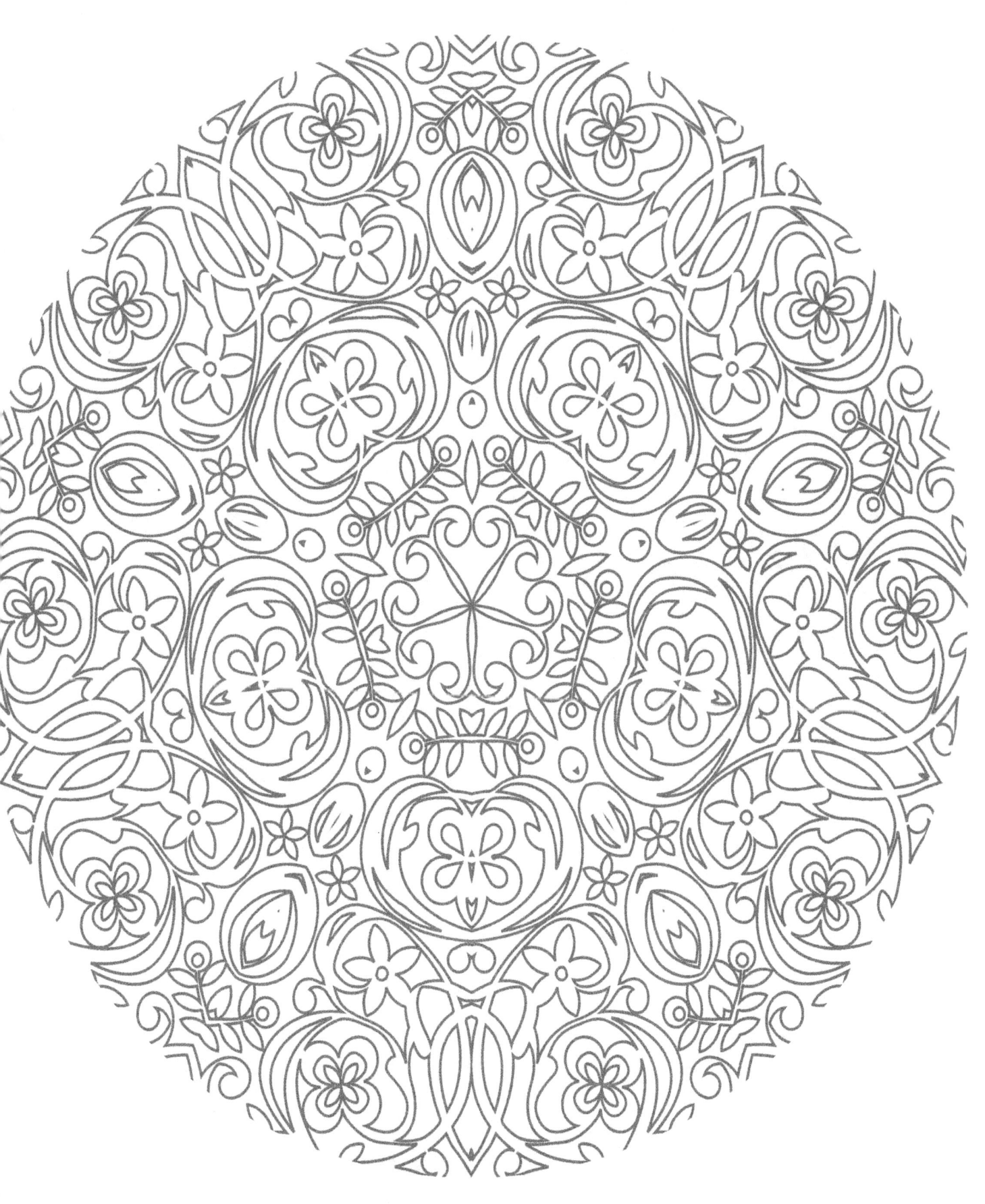

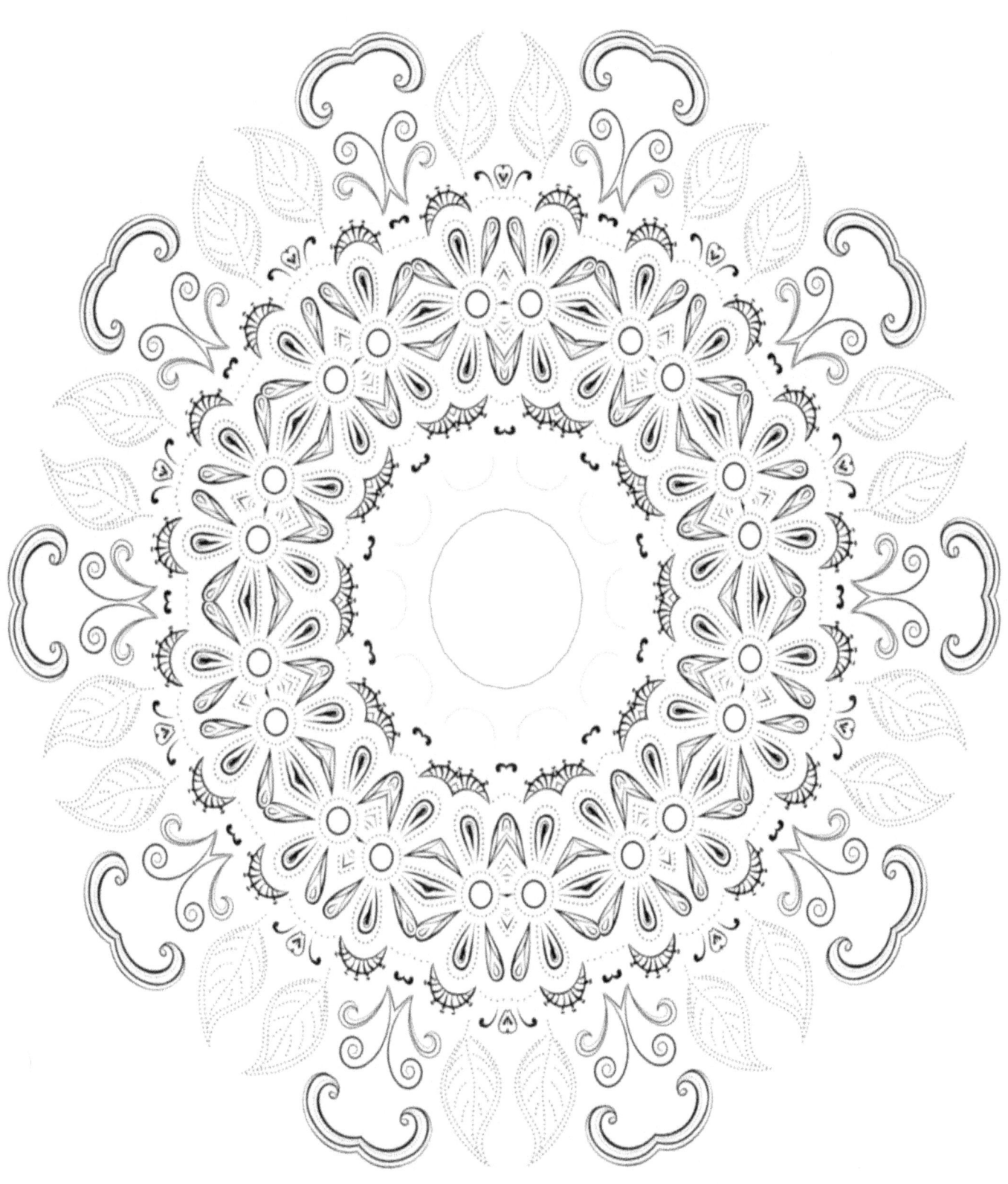

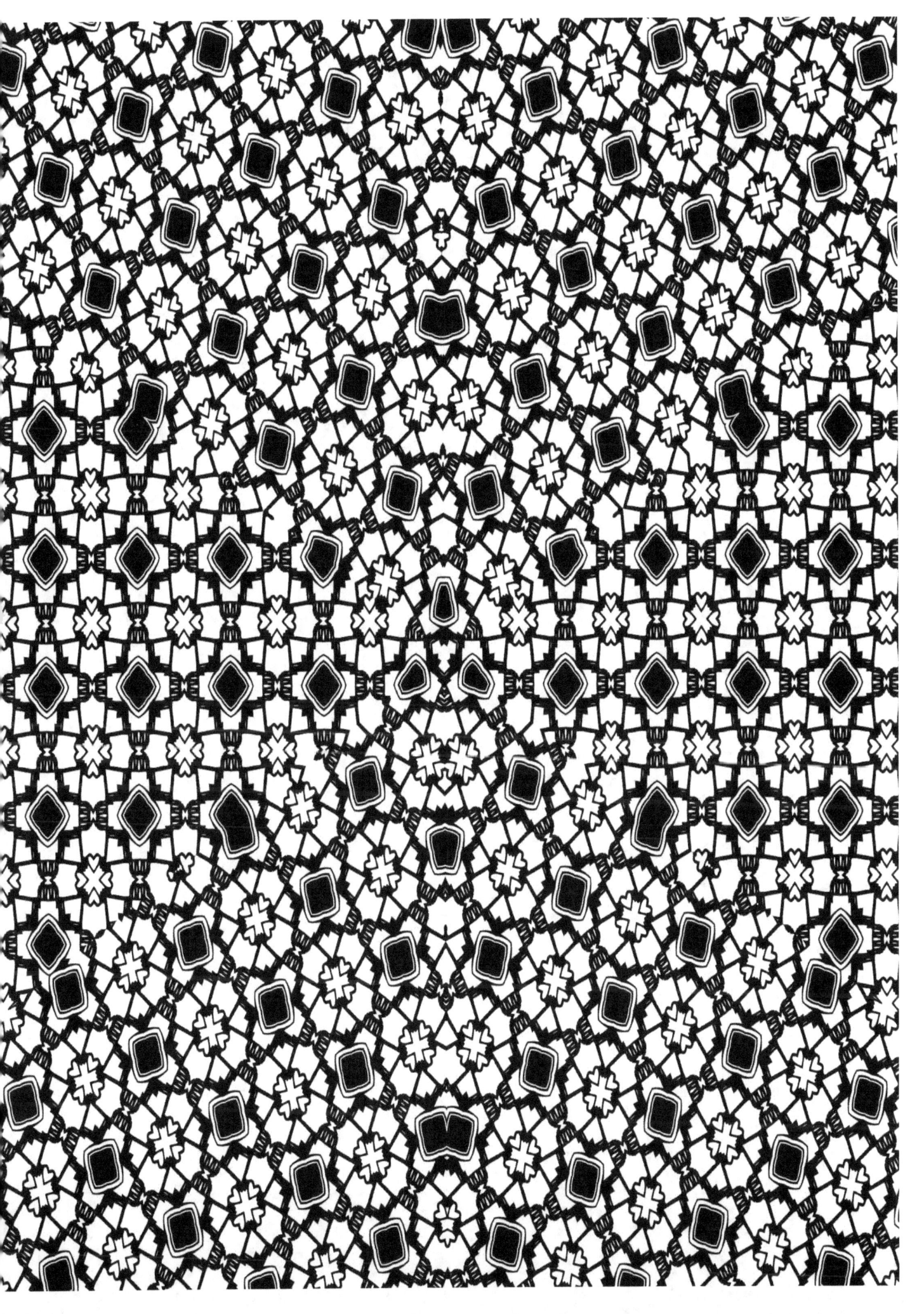

I hope you have enjoyed coloring this book and you found the relaxation you were looking for. Feel free to send a comment or a completed picture to dsgnbymelissa@gmail.com. I look forward to hearing from you and keep your eye out for more coloring books and journals!

www.ingramcontent.com/pod-product-compliance
Lightning Source LLC
Chambersburg PA
CBHW062158220526
45470CB00009B/2864